Life in Time

Life in Time

Jodi Brown Wentzell

All rights reserved. No part of this book may be reproduced, stored, or transmitted by any means, whether auditory, graphic, mechanical, or electronic without written permission of both publisher and author, except in the case of brief excerpts used in critical articles and reviews. Unauthorized reproduction of any part of this work is illegal and is punishable by law.

Copyright © 2022 Jodi Brown Wentzell

ISBN 13: 978-1-944662-73-8

Publishing date: June 2022

This is a work of fiction. Names, characters, businesses, places, events and incidents are either the products of the author's imagination or are used in a fictitious manner. Any resemblance to actual persons, living or dead, or actual events is purely coincidental.

Cover Design by Diana Henderson © 2022

Dedication

Dedicated to:

My daughter Mandy Lynn. You are my sunshine.

To Lillian and Thomas for letting me experience the kind of Love that people freely die for.

To my family and friends for bringing me to myself. Mom, I Love you for teaching me the power of writing out your emotions. Dad, your guiding Spirit is my true north.

My Beloved Chris whose friendship, Love and support through the years is a blessing beyond measure. It has allowed me to not only rise but to shine.

To Love. The root of all bliss and blues.

Poetry,

    Spiritual Script,

        Metaphysics Phrase

            And

                Words of Wisdom...

Table of Contents

Dedication v
Grande Illusion 1
Untitled #1 7
Untitled #2 9
Untitled #3 11
Untitled #4 13
Untitled #5 17
Untitled #6 19
Untitled #7 21
A Season 23
Untitled #8 25
Oh when you touch me 27
Untitled #9 31
Untitled #10 33
Untitled #11 35
Untitled #12 37
Untitled #13 39
Untitled #14 41
Untitled #15 43

Untitled #16 45
Untitled #17 47
Untitled #18 49
Untitled #19 51
Untitled #20 53
Untitled #21 55
Untitled #22 57
Questions 59
Untitled #23 61
Untitled #24 63
Untitled #25 65
When Time is Shown 67
Untitled #26 69
Untitled #27 71
Untitled #28 73
Untitled #29 75
Untitled #30 77
Untitled #31 79
Untitled #32 81
Untitled #33 83
Untitled #34 85

Untitled #35 87

Untitled #36 89

Untitled #37 91

Untitled #38 93

Untitled #39 95

Untitled #40 97

Untitled #41 99

Untitled #42 101

Untitled #43 103

Untitled #44 105

Untitled #45 107

Untitled #46 109

Untitled #47 111

Untitled #48 113

Untitled #49 115

Untitled #50 117

Untitled #51 119

Untitled #52 121

Untitled #53 123

Untitled #54 125

Untitled #55 127

Untitled #56 129

Untitled #57 131

Untitled #58 133

Untitled #59 135

Untitled #60 137

Untitled #61 139

Untitled #62 141

Untitled #63 143

Untitled #64 145

Untitled #65 147

Untitled #66 149

Untitled #67 151

Untitled #68 153

Untitled #69 155

Untitled #70 157

Untitled #71 159

Untitled #72 161

Untitled #73 163

Untitled #74 165

Untitled #75 167

Mornin' Missin' You 169

The World We Believe 171
Loves Chime 173
Untitled #76 175
The Path of Loves Grace 177
Prayer of the Beloved.. 179
The Dedication... 181
The Wrap... 183

Grande Illusion

The words speak of living,
A world without giving.
Tell of a game,
One with no name.
Hoping people will know
It's been made a show.

No lead part!
Well, break my heart.
What will be seen,
On that great giant screen.
Was that really me,
What's that I see?
If I could be anything,
That's what it would be.

How wonderful was it to be
In the book of History.
The story does tell,

Life in Time

My wishes I made in the well.
What would I do,
Wearing a shoe.

In the final cut,
Won't see a nut.
Agony was reality,
Glad it felt good to me.

When time tells all,
There is no rise or fall
I can say what I see,
Sure good to me.

Have no pain,
What is a name.
Is that all I get for playing
The Game.

Life in Time

What time will tell,
If you'd really rather, hell.
Heaven is nice,
The very best price.

So good to see
You're here with me.
To have a friend,
In the end.
I Love you so,
But surely, you know.
You love me back,
I saw in the show.
Caused me no pain,
All through the rain,
Glad you saw the sun,
It sure was fun.

Life in Time

Look at the hurt
Living on plain dirt.
You took some pain
Out of that gain.

Sure sorry to see,
They're not here with me.
With all the rain,
Never saw the sane.

So glad you care,
Life really was fair.
Love is the fare,
That gets you there.

Life in Time

Safely through the sea,
Of life, reality.
The ride, The otherside,
Ecstasy to me.
With you my friend,
I'm happy to be.
No Bitter end,
In this show I see.

Life in Time

Untitled #1

Walk with me a while,
Help me make the mile.
And to you I will send,
A Love that will never end.

Untitled #2

When all seems to fail,
can't find the trail, of
what makes your heart happy.
Just look to the sun,
And remember the fun
Of your yesterdays.

Untitled #3

Why fight?
Doesn't feel right,
Have a hand to hold,
Yet still be so cold.
Some will never see
Through the mystery—
Of Love.

Life in Time

Untitled #4

My heart burning
as flames of the sun.
My soul yearning
for you, the One.

So the fire does roll and wave
my Spirit dizzy, does love save?
Sometimes I wonder,
Don't know why.
Is love real,
Or really just the lie.

I can wallow in splendor
and dwell in waste,
Can see love's beauty,
and enjoy the taste.

Life in Time

Can't understand,
everything turin' to paste.

Pieces of paper made of wood,
Over the Soul's eyes,
God! What a hood.
Gotta see the way,
and know it's the day
when everything's comin' up roses.

My visions can't be
Mass-produced,
Or sold at Uncle Bill's.
But wouldn't trade the thrills,
Nor forget the chills.

Life in Time

My Soul burning
as flames on the sun,
My heart knowing
Now I Am the One.

Life in Time

Untitled #5

Say I think to much,
Can't see the day,
Then say I don't think enough,
Can't find my way.

But watch as you see me,
On my way out.
Gettin' away from you,
I've seen what you're about.

Don't tell me no more—
as I head for a door,
Not gonna stay around
Not gonna be your floor.

Untitled #6

I'm fading fast
Don't think I can last,
My star that burns bright
Somehow shows no light.
Lost in the night
of a time gone past.
Nowhere is somewhere,
And doing nothing means a lot.
Don't want to be a slave no more,
Gonna break this law—
Gonna find Ecstasy,
One that all can see
And all will be free.
Cause I have been there my friend
To a where there is no end.
Where happiness is in the breeze
And there is no need to let it be.
Yeah, I wanna break this law
And make a better place,

Life in Time

Where everyone can have paradise.
Wanna fill the hole—
The spot in the soul—
that holds everyone.
If I could only fill the grave,
that hides the light of our day
Then we could see it is no mystery—
We are in heaven.
Please won't you help me,
I thought you were my friend—
Don't wanna see a bitter end,
Or have to begin again.
Just want to feel—
Love that is real.
My friend what you can't see
is you and me,
Would be peace and harmony.

Life in Time

Untitled #7

When I go don't say goodbye
Just a hug and a sigh,
You should know why,
Gotta lift my Spirit high.

I played my hand,
Met the Band
and saved my soul
By rock 'n' roll.

All through the night
Music felt so right.
Took the pain,
From the gain.
And you gotta know,
It was a hell of a show.

Life in Time

A Season

*I wouldn't put down your friends or clientele
no more than you would put down mine.
Just as you for me!
But I will always say that goodbye came too soon.
As it always does.
Thank you so much for everything I learned,
and for the love you showed me.
I will never forget the play.
And so I grow to a woman from a child,
but still I knew all the while, you were not mine,
but I guess no one can define,
the good I know comes in time,
But, ah, you my love were a season,
one that only rewinds in my mind.
But now I realize the time,
for I only see, that you don't love the me!
Only the myself and I
and that is why, we,
Must say goodbye!*

Life in Time

Untitled #8

*As real as a Rainbow
 that wraps up the sky,
As good as the feeling
when the spirit's free to fly.
As wonderful as Heaven
the ultimate of high—
You'll find no lost space,
but always the intimacy of place,
and your face will always
be a pleasure to me.*

*If ever the hill gets steep
or battle long,
You can always come home to sleep,
and let your will grow strong.
In a home that's made of love,
you're never right or wrong*

Life in Time

cause no matter how you feel,
there you still belong.
Never have a leader to
tell you what to do,
But a friend to help you
find what feels best to you.
Never find a maid nor wench
Only someone kind
No, never a game to cause you pain,
Love that has no bind.
Just a place you can stretch,
where peace you can find.
For your spirit and mind,
Your soul to find rest.

Life in Time

Oh when you touch me

*You send a thrill all
through my spine,
 Just with anticipation
of knowing you are mine.*

 *And to me you do deliver,
the certain sense of quiver,
that is more precious than gold,
no matter how old.
 And I hope one day you'll see
the special love you bring to me—
knowing all the time I'm there
to love you and to care!*

*"But Oh when you touch me—
nothing is a mystery,
a pleasure I can not find—
No matter how far I look behind"*

Life in Time

   And for making my life worth time
in knowing that you are mine,
will always get me through—
No matter what you say or do.
   Because, Oh when you touch me
there's nothing I can not see.
A certain sense of victory,
in knowing that you're touching me.

   You can show the way
of taking out the grey,
and making everyday seem clear
in knowing that your near,
No matter how far you are.

Life in Time

Because, Oh when you touch me—
what my eyes cannot see,
lies in my Spirit, as though part of me—
and sends a rush of senses,
that has no chains or fences.
For you make life fun to live,
and make it all worth the give!

"But Oh when you touch me
nothing is a mystery,
a pleasure I cannot find—
No matter how far I look behind."

Life in Time

Untitled #9

*Your eyes of marble,
the kind I always wanted—
Your hair trimmed in gold,
the kind I've always hunted.*

Life in Time

Untitled #10

*No bars can hold
a spirit so free
or chains can take
the love in me.
With God by my side
I'll take the ride
and soon, will go home.*

Life in Time

Untitled #11

I love you so
You'll never know.
But no matter how far—
My love as a star
Will shine on you.

Life in Time

Untitled #12

A love so true,
The skies so blue,
Gives the clue—
That this is Heaven.

Life in Time

Untitled #13

Love, melt the bars,
My eyes see stars,
To smell the air,
And feel life fair,
You and I will soar,
Into evermore.

Life in Time

Untitled #14

*Like a child
finding buried treasure,
In you—
I will pleasure!*

Life in Time

Untitled #15

Like a bird flying free
Soon I will be!
Then you will see
The real me.

Life in Time

Untitled #16

I can give you gain
or I can cause you pain
I can give you pleasure
And large amounts of buried treasure
But you must let me be
what is really me
Or never will you see
the love that is in me

Life in Time

Untitled #17

I'm not what you want,
No, I'm not a cunt
Ain't gonna play the game,
Don't need the mental pain.

Life in Time

Untitled #18

Why do you gotta be like this
Treating me as a fish,
As soon as you make the catch
Then you make the kill,
I think it's called mental ill
You don't know what love is about—
All you want is your trout.

Untitled #19

Can't be myself
sitting on your mental shelf
I must be free
Free to be me
Why can't you see
There is no feel
In a love that's unreal
No glory, or no gain
Just pain in a game
Can't play a roll
Don't want to pay the toll
So I will go my on my way
And to you I say...
Goodbye!

Life in Time

Untitled #20

Wanna get high,
I wanna fly
Wanna bust through these bars,
Wanna see stars.
Wanna run with the wind
and watch the world spin
Wanna see love grow
the kind that I know
Don't wanna watch the world go by . . .
No, I want to fly

Life in Time

Untitled #21

*Through the bars I can see
a great spectacular sunset.
Could it be, what I see
Is just for me—
A gift from God, to let me know
my soul still free.
Oh, could it be just for me?
And God said to me
No Matter where I go
I should know
He will be with me.*

Life in Time

Untitled #22

So excuse me if I may seem crude;
But life has shown me the sides of rude.
I saw the cold and felt the pain;
And many have tried to take my brain.
But yet I go on loving the chill of the cold,
and finding pleasure within the pain.
And in my mind I can see
the sunshine in the rain.

Some say I'm crazy,
others think I'm just plain lazy,
But I don't complain as
long as music can ease my brain,
I can smile in my pain,
Make the hurt go away,
the intensity of feeling moves in to stay.

Life in Time

Oh sooth my soul and calm my body,
let me rest in your Rock 'n' Roll.
You can fill my need, and
love from my heart can freely bleed.

The rush of the flow,
just lets me know that
Love is real, the kind I feel.
Takes away my fear—
Of the end that's near.

Life in Time

Questions

Sometimes it seems,
just a fading star—
giving it's last glow.
Showing what I know
before I burn out.
Know what it's about
Still light can't be seen.
And the glow dies to
A stream of hope.

Your question: nope, dope,
or the Pope.
Where do you think you are?
Do you think Heaven is a star?
Look as far as you can see—
And still not realize it is to be.

Life in Time

And still go for—
what is never more!
Don't feel reality, just the pain
of others ugly gain.
And still don't see—
It is just a game.

Life in Time

Untitled #23

Waiting for you,
What more can one do?
Know what I want,
Yes I can see.
And what it is,
For you with me.
Still your not home,
And I'm here alone.
Why can't you see
how you feel to me?

Life in Time

Untitled #24

*Jealousy is no more—
Than the fear that Love
is not real.*

Untitled #25

I hope these words to say
the way I really feel.
One of a love that is real.
It comes far inside from
the only place I have to hide.
An intimate and warm spot
that burns inside endlessly.
And all around is empty
space needing to be filled.
The scars and the stars
from the places I've been,
Still continue again and again
In a sweet harmonious refrain.
Looking for a love, pure and true.
One of a passion of pleasure and life.
A soul to lift my spirits so I can fly,
and then will see the ultimate high.

Life in Time

When Time is Shown

What is real? What I feel?
Or is it all pain? Just a gain?
Down the drain? Is it all sane?
Is it rain? Or just a game?
Where to go? Can love grow?
What will be known?
When time is shown?

Life in Time

Untitled #26

Life is funny; skies are sunny;
Thought you were poor;
Always wanting more;
Why can't it be;
Me for you, and you for me

Life in Time

Untitled #27

Can I love you
Is it sane?
Or is it all
for mental pain?

Untitled #28

With you my soul has found
the love of yours and the contentment
of peace within another soul.

In my mind I have found
love with your mind and
my person loves your person as well.
But the love I have for you in spirit and soul
is so pure it could never be stained.
It is immaculate.
And I will hold it as such for eternity.

None can compare to the beauty and trust
I have found in you, one above all others.
One so true and real that no bad can try to rust.
For it is gold, of the purest form.

Life in Time

Untitled #29

*You have a friend,
from beginning to end.
And after forever
No matter the weather,
You'll never be alone
for in my heart you have a home.
And when you're down
I hope you know I'm around.*

Life in Time

Untitled #30

Living on a merry-go-round
Sometimes makes one dizzy.

Life in Time

Untitled #31

I thank all for your kindness,
and appreciation of what I have to offer.
And would like to say,
that your music is the ultimate feeling to me.
Truthfully it is the best of anything
I have ever in my life felt.
And for that I will always be true.

No matter where you are or however far,
My hope for your happiness will always be.

Life in Time

Untitled #32

The truth hurts, don't it!
When the truth hurts,
You're not be truthful
With your self.

Life in Time

Untitled #33

Judgement Day is merely the memories that you make with life.

Life in Time

Untitled #34

*As long as what you're doing is good—
It can't be bad
And nothing can change that!*

Life in Time

Untitled #35

*My heart pounds, and a
chill flows up my spine,
for in you I have found,
a friend that is mine.
I want to Love you, but
can't take the chance;
of losing a friend to find romance.*

Life in Time

Untitled #36

Don't know your game,
not sure I want to play.
Although you go,
I still stay, just on a wish
that you'll come my way.
You make me feel better
than anything can compare.
Yet our moments we do not share.
Is it worth the pain?
Will love be the gain?
Or will nothing remain?

Life in Time

Untitled #37

Do you love her, does she care?
When it all comes down will she still be there?
I need you so, you'll never know.
Why must this love not show?
Why can't you be here with me?

Life in Time

Untitled #38

You made my dream so happy and true,
The only one that's not fulfilled,
Is that I can't have you.

Untitled #39

I find my heart to be
loyal and true,
Yet deep in my soul I'm
lonely and blue.
I've traveled through time
to find someone like you,
only to realize my dream
can't come true.

So I'll travel along like
so many times before.
But I pray that someday,
I may find your door.

Life in Time

Untitled #40

*You possess a part of me
beyond reason and doubt,
a power so deep you can
not talk about.
For no words can say,
the feeling we are sharing
and the magic of its way
just being together and
sharing the day.*

Life in Time

Untitled #41

*The only real man is
one who knows how to treat
a real woman,
Is one that understands the
child, girl, lady and woman in one,
and love each with the
feeling of love.*

Untitled #42

When we are all dead and gone,
I hope I can always be on ...
your side.
For I hope that you will see,
the love you put in me.
And I wish it to be said,
that our love will never be dead.

Life in Time

Untitled #43

*The knowledge of a woman—
with the brave and pounding
heart of a child.
Oh, how I love you!*

Life in Time

Untitled #44

I Love you so much,
Nothing can compare
A feeling of such
Will always be there.

Life in Time

Untitled #45

*For nothing can compare
to the sound of a baby's cry,
And for those who cannot try,
still ask why—
For they do not see eternity,
But I can see you, and
you can see me.*

Life in Time

Untitled #46

For if I should grow old,
with the story of life untold...
I hope that you will see
the glow you put in me.

Life in Time

Untitled #47

As the sound of silence
flows through your mind,
like rapid flowing blood
with every feeling unturned,
and everything understood.

Life in Time

Untitled #48

*Through the trials
you make the miles
Seem like minutes to me.*

Life in Time

Untitled #49

I hope some day will show;
That Love can only grow.
And so throughout history,
No mystery or misery,
Just love you see.

Life in Time

Untitled #50

Life can't be against us I feel;
For only love is really real.

Life in Time

Untitled #51

*And your certain little glow,
I've come to love and know,
will always show, love is real.*

Life in Time

Untitled #52

It really hurts to say good-bye—
It's hard to believe it was just a lie.
It hurts so bad that I just want to cry,
How can we let a love like ours die—

Life in Time

Untitled #53

*First you're up and then you're down,
Why can't you see it goes around*

Untitled #54

Paradise to me is something
I believe I'll see.
I don't know what will be,
But I'm sure when I'm there, I'm
sure I'll know what's where.

I just wish that there you'll be
to share and add to the ecstasy.

Life in Time

Untitled #55

Dear God I thank you for
this day, and for not letting
all time be wasted away.
I thank you for your Love
and special way of getting
me through each day.
I can only pray, that you'll
allow me to return the Love
to you each day and
feel the greatest feeling only
you control.
The one that I've come to know,
I hope to me you'll always show.
For all the feelings there are
to know, Love is the only one
that will make my soul glow;
And may it always be that way,
My Spirit in Heaven will lay.

                   - *Amen*

Life in Time

Untitled #56

Though tired you may be,
I hope it sets you free.
Cause then your eyes will see
that you can let it be, and
we are here for you and me.

Life in Time

Untitled #57

*No material thing can show
the beauty in you I've come
 to know.
You want to go, but I want
you to stay—
I guess that's just my way
of saying—
I Love you!*

Life in Time

Untitled #58

*I need you to hold me
in the black of night.
Then I will see,
that all is right.*

Life in Time

Untitled #59

*You wonder if you should,
and really rather would
You know you could;
But just sit and wonder
if you should.*

*I know that love is real,
cause I my love can feel
the pure and simple ecstasy
of a Spirit that is free.*

*Have no fear of pain,
Nor need of gain.
For it's here you will see,
is where love is meant to be.*

Life in Time

Come on set me free
Let them all be.
Then we will soon see,
Total Ecstasy.

Life in Time

Untitled #60

Your life is shit,
Your game's a trip—
Thought you were more,
But your only poor.
You may have style
But you got no class,
And all in all,
You're just a pain in the ass.
What breaks my heart,
is you're such a waste—
a thing of beauty
full of disgrace.
Better quit your game,
or you will see—
All you were was a misery.

Life in Time

Untitled #61

You can never recapture
a moment—or even refeel
a feeling.
 Games have no end—
either you quit, or you
eat shit and die.

Life in Time

Untitled #62

And for all on the ego trip
will not find an end,
For there is no road
that leads there,
In the end to be a dip
in shit.

Life in Time

Untitled #63

You never realize what it is;
till you see it as a loss.

Life in Time

Untitled #64

*My heart is aching,
feels like it's breaking.
Gave you my heart,
Gave you my soul,
Gave all my power to
your rock and roll.
But did you ever call,
or even care?
Took all I had for
you to see me there.*

*But you didn't see
how much I care,
Gave you all I had.
Can't ask for more—
But it's just a laugh
from one on the floor.*

Life in Time

Before I move on,
and travel along—
Just want you to know—
That I truly loved the show.

Life in Time

Untitled #65

*Jails should be used
to sharpen a person's senses.
Instead a person is
forced to lose them.*

Life in Time

Untitled #66

*What I really wish
everyone would realize—
Is that sense and feeling
are the same thing.*

Life in Time

Untitled #67

Some thing is better than no thing, cause at least it's there.

Life in Time

Untitled #68

God didn't make men strong
Because women need carried,
He gave them feet as well.
And He didn't give man logic
Because women need thought,
but gave women feelings
so men could have something
to find a way of figuring
out how to do it.

Life in Time

Untitled #69

*God made man woman
so he would have something to do.
With the world as it is Today,
It's a shame he doesn't
Know he should like it.*

*When He gave him the
nicest thing that could be,
All he's doing is trying to
think of ways not to like it.*

Life in Time

Untitled #70

A wimp is the worst thing
in the world a man can be.
A whore is the worst
kind of woman that could be.
We should see—
Both of which caused by agony.

Life in Time

Untitled #71

*You can tell what kind
of person a man is,
by the way he takes care
of his woman.*

Life in Time

Untitled #72

I'm sick of living,
Sick of trying,
Sick of losing,
Sick of dying.

Life in Time

Untitled #73

*If you really want fun,
it's second to none!
How much can you take,
See how much more you can make.*

Life in Time

Untitled #74

I hope someday you'll see,
You are the star I see,
And I hope someday
You will be...
The only love for me!

Life in Time

Untitled #75

God is with me,
God is with you,
God is anywhere that
You want him to!

Life in Time

Mornin' Missin' You

The world and all its treasures,
And all its simple pleasures—
I believe that I will see no finer;
Than the likes of you—

Life in Time

The World We Believe

How things are
How they will be ...
Really depend on you
and me.

And how love can grow
And what we are to know,
Can only be seen through
our eyes as we see it.

Life in Time

Loves Chime

The church bells glare,
in my mind do stare,
A vision of light—
all through the night.
Lets you know that love
is there ...
  In the air
To see young loves on the
streets holding hands,
all through the lands
and deep in our souls,
We wish for it one in all—

For no greater love can
there be ...
Than to have you with me.
To hear the bells chime
And think of the time
Oh the love you send to me.

Life in Time

Untitled #76

There sat a man
with a frightening glare.
But as I approached him,
in the glimpse of a stare,
The glare turned to a glow,
and I was to know.
That there, happiness
can be found.

Life in Time

The Path of Loves Grace

Through miles uncounted
Emotions unnamed—
An unrefrained melody
In harmony unchained—
Trust was lost
and then regained—
Shared laughter and smiles
through hidden fears—
Joy, comfort and warmth
known in the years—
Feeling Loves glow
through unseen tears—
We travel this road
Rocky but True—
For Love is our Home
Found within us two—

Life in Time

The safety of shelter
with the stress of repairs—
No matter the weather
Our sorrows and cares—
Love which stands strong
We will belong together
The path we travel along

Life in Time

Prayer of the Beloved

Please light my way,
with a shimmering glow.
Please help me to grow
and know what I am to know.
Please keep me strong,
so I do no wrong.
Please keep me well,
for it is in your Hands my soul lies.
Please keep me in the light of your Love,
for there, is no doubt or fear,
nor darkness.
May I walk at your side,
                Always.
      ·   *-Amen*

Life in Time

The Dedication

Dedicated to the Love within—
To those we love now and then...
No matter how close or far apart
There is a piece of the Love
Forever etched in our heart
Long ago or today,
In my heart it will always stay

Life in Time

The Wrap

Our paths we crossed
We draw the line
And I must say,
The time was fine.

As we move on in time
A simple joy in knowing
That once you were mine.

So to you my special friend,
The love that's ours will never end.

I wish there were more
But that's what time is for
To move along,
Sing another song.
For now no need to cry,
To you as I say goodbye.

www.ingramcontent.com/pod-product-compliance
Lightning Source LLC
Chambersburg PA
CBHW030151100526
44592CB00009B/216